The Glittering World of Gems

SPARKLING SAPPHIRES

By Joyce Jeffries

KidHaven PUBLISHING

Published in 2018 by
KidHaven Publishing, an Imprint of Greenhaven Publishing, LLC
353 3rd Avenue
Suite 255
New York, NY 10010

Designer: Seth Hughes
Editor: Vanessa Oswald

Photo credits: Cover (left) Albert Russ/Shutterstock.com; cover (right) TinaImages/Shutterstock.com; cover, pp. 2, 4, 6, 8, 10, 12, 14, 16, 18, 20–21, back cover (background) ILeysen/Shutterstock.com; p. 5 © iStockphoto.com/YolandaVanNiekerk; p. 7 Dennis van de Water/Shutterstock.com; p. 9 © Shepard Sherbell/CORBIS SABA/Corbis via Getty Images; p. 11 BIOPHOTO ASSOCIATES/Science Source/Getty Images; p.13 Imfoto/Shutterstock.com; p. 15 SunChan/E+/Getty Images; p. 17 ryasick/E+/Getty Images; p. 19 Pisut Phaetrangsee/Shutterstock.com; p. 20 (top) Magnus Manske/Wikimedia Commons; p. 20 (bottom) Chatsam/Wikimedia Commons; p. 21 (top) Ra'ike/Wikimedia Commons; p. 21 (bottom) Arthur Edwards - WPA Pool/Getty Images.

Cataloging-in-Publication Data

Names: Jeffries, Joyce.
Title: Sparkling sapphires / Joyce Jeffries.
Description: New York : KidHaven Publishing, 2018. | Series: The glittering world of gems | Includes index.
Identifiers: ISBN 9781534523128 (pbk.) | 9781534523074 (library bound) | ISBN 9781534522978 (6 pack) | ISBN 9781534523029 (ebook)
Subjects: LCSH: Sapphires–Juvenile literature.
Classification: LCC QE394.S3 J43 2018 | DDC 553.8'4–dc23

Printed in the United States of America

CPSIA compliance information: Batch #BS17KL: For further information contact Greenhaven Publishing LLC, New York, New York at 1-844-317-7404.

Please visit our website, www.greenhavenpublishing.com. For a free color catalog of all our high-quality books, call toll free 1-844-317-7404 or fax 1-844-317-7405.

CONTENTS

What Are Sapphires Made From?	4
Sapphire Mining	6
Mining Machines	8
Finding Raw Sapphires	10
Sapphires of Many Colors	12
Creating Sapphire Jewelry	14
Heat Treating and Setting Sapphires	16
What Makes a Sapphire Valuable?	18
Glossary	22
For More Information	23
Index	24

WHAT ARE SAPPHIRES MADE FROM?

Sapphires are a form of the **mineral** corundum. These gems are **transparent**, and most are a deep blue color. Pure corundum is colorless and mostly made of the element aluminum. The reason sapphires are blue is because small amounts of the elements iron and titanium are mixed in.

Not all sapphires are blue, but this is the most common color. Yellow and green sapphires are sometimes found in nature.

Mining for Facts!

Sapphires are hard gems. The only gems that are harder are diamonds!

Sapphires are added to **jewelry** such as these necklaces.

SAPPHIRE MINING

Sapphire **deposits** are found all over the world in places such as Sri Lanka, Madagascar, Myanmar, Kashmir, and Thailand. In the town of Ilakaka, Madagascar, a very large gem-**quality** sapphire deposit was discovered in 1998. People mined this area for sapphires and made fortunes.

Sri Lanka is now the world's biggest supplier of sapphires. Sapphires are generally found near the surface of the ground. Sometimes sapphires aren't easy to mine, and mining can be dangerous. The easiest way to mine sapphires is by using hand tools, but sometimes miners have to dig deep tunnels in hard rock and use heavy machines.

Mining for Facts!

Australia was considered the largest producer of sapphires until 1987.

Shown here is a large sapphire mine in Madagascar.

MINING MACHINES

After big machines take large amounts of rocks and dirt out of the ground, the miners use other machines to wash these piles. The piles are sorted into big and small pieces and then put into a machine called a pulsator. The pulsator shakes the rocks, and the heavier ones fall to the bottom. This is generally where sapphires are found. These stones are then sorted to find gem-quality sapphires.

Big mining companies are able to find more sapphires since they have better machines. However, sometimes they throw out good sapphires with waste rock, and some people have found sapphires in the waste piles.

Large machines such as this one are often used for sapphire mining.

FINDING RAW SAPPHIRES

Before a sapphire becomes shiny and ready to be made into jewelry, it's raw and dull. Newly mined sapphires are most often blue, green, or yellow. To find gem-quality sapphires, large amounts of dirt and rocks need to be mined and sorted.

It can be hard to spot sapphires mixed in with rocks and dirt. Miners dig through small amounts of rocks at a time. After this, they wash the rocks on screens. Once this is done, it's easier for miners to find sapphires.

Mining for Facts!

Sapphire is the birthstone for the month of September.

Shown here is a cut sapphire on the left next to a raw, uncut sapphire on the right.

SAPPHIRES OF MANY COLORS

Sapphires come in many different colors. Most sapphires are a deep blue color, but there are also "fancy sapphires." These sapphires can be yellow, green, pink, or colorless. Sometimes jewelers will use colorless sapphires instead of diamonds in jewelry. The gems look like diamonds but are less expensive.

Pink-orange sapphires are a very **rare** and **valuable** kind of sapphire found in Sri Lanka. The only color a sapphire can't be is red. Then it would be considered a ruby, which is red-colored corundum.

Mining for Facts!

There are also black sapphires. These are the least transparent.

This raw pink sapphire is very rare and valuable!

CREATING SAPPHIRE JEWELRY

Before a raw sapphire can be made into **sparkling** jewelry, a jeweler called a lapidary uses a diamond-tipped saw with a lot of water to cut it from the raw crystal. Next, the lapidary shapes the stone by **grinding** flat surfaces called facets into it.

Star sapphires show a six-pointed star when looked at under a bright light. This kind of sapphire is generally cut and **polished** into a round or oval mound shape. Gem cutters choose these shapes because they're the easiest to make and show off the star pattern the best.

Mining for Facts!

Sapphires display brighter colors when viewed at different angles.

Shown here is a star sapphire that's been placed into a piece of jewelry.

HEAT TREATING AND SETTING SAPPHIRES

A sapphire may have tiny flaws, called inclusions, in it before it's given to a lapidary to shape and polish. To get rid of most of these inclusions, the sapphires are heat treated.

Once a sapphire is heat treated, it's placed in a metal setting of gold or silver. To place the metal setting around the faceted gem, sapphires are held in place by small hooks called prongs. These prongs curve around the edges of the finished stone.

This gold ring has a large sapphire and diamonds that make it very valuable.

WHAT MAKES A SAPPHIRE VALUABLE?

Many things decide a sapphire's value. The most important features of a sapphire are its cut, color, **clarity**, and size.

Facets are cut into a sapphire to make it shine its brightest when put under light, making it very valuable. Completely flawless sapphires are very rare and have the highest value. Most sapphires have a few inclusions, but the ones that have fewer are worth more. Larger gems with a higher carat weight are more valuable. The weight of a gem is measured in carats. One carat is equal to 0.007 ounce (200 mg).

Mining for Facts!

Blue to violet-blue sapphires are the most valuable.

A jeweler can cut a sapphire into many different sizes!

FAMOUS SAPPHIRES

What: Star of India, which is the largest gem-quality blue sapphire

When: formed 2 billion years ago, discovered about 300 years ago

Where: The Star of India was found in Sri Lanka. In 1900, J.P. Morgan presented the sapphire to the American Museum of Natural History, where it still is today.

Weight: 563 carats (112.6 g)

Value: unknown

What: Black Star of Queensland, which is one of the largest gem-quality star sapphires

When: It was found by a 12-year-old boy in the 1930s. It was used as a doorstop in his family's home for years before being sold to jeweler Harry Kazanjian in 1947.

Where: Queensland, Australia

Weight: 733 carats (146.6 g)

Value: more than $80 million

What: Logan Sapphire, which is one of the largest faceted blue sapphires

When: Mrs. Rebecca Logan, who the sapphire is named after, donated the sapphire to the Smithsonian Institution in 1960.

Where: found in Sri Lanka

Weight: 423 carats (84.6 g)

Value: unknown

What: royal sapphire engagement ring

When: This sapphire engagement ring was chosen by England's Princess Diana in 1981. Her son William presented it to Kate Middleton in 2010.

Where: found in Sri Lanka

Weight: 12 carats (2.4 g)

Value: $300,000

Mining for Facts!

The Star of India and the Delong Star Ruby were stolen in 1964. The gems, which were valued at more than $400,000, were found and the thieves were caught a year later.

GLOSSARY

clarity: The state of being clear.

deposit: An amount of a mineral in the ground that built up over a period of time.

grind: To shape or smooth something with a rough surface.

jewelry: Pieces of metal, often holding gems, that are worn on the body.

mineral: A natural, solid substance that is not a plant or animal.

polish: To rub something with a soft cloth to make it smooth and shiny.

quality: The standard of something.

rare: Not seen very often.

sparkle: To give off flashes of light.

transparent: Easily seen through.

valuable: Having great worth.

FOR MORE INFORMATION

Websites

Gem Kids: Sapphire
gemkids.gia.edu/gem/sapphire
This website includes fun facts about sapphires.

National Geographic Kids: Sapphire
kids.nationalgeographic.com/explore/science/sapphire/#sapphire-raw.jpg
Visitors to this website can find cool photos and information on sapphires.

Books

Green, Dan. *The Rock and Gem Book: A Visual Encyclopedia of the Earth's Treasures.* New York, NY: DK Publishing, 2016.

Hansen, Grace. *Gems.* Minneapolis, MN: ABDO Kids, 2016.

Publisher's note to educators and parents: Our editors have carefully reviewed these websites to ensure that they are suitable for students. Many websites change frequently, however, and we cannot guarantee that a site's future contents will continue to meet our high standards of quality and educational value. Be advised that students should be closely supervised whenever they access the Internet.

INDEX

A

Australia, 6, 20

C

carat, 18, 20, 21
clarity, 18
color, 4, 12, 14, 18
corundum, 4, 12
crystal, 14
cut, 11, 14, 18, 19

F

facet, 14, 16, 18, 21
fancy sapphires, 12

I

inclusions, 16, 18

J

jewelry, 5, 10, 12, 14, 15

L

lapidary, 14, 16

M

Madagascar, 6, 7
miners, 6, 8, 10

P

polish, 14, 16
prongs, 16
pulsator, 8

S

Sri Lanka, 6, 12, 20, 21
star sapphires, 14, 15, 20, 21

T

transparent, 4, 12